LYNYRD SKYNYRD

CONTENTS

Title	Page
Working For MCA	5
I Ain't The One	8
Searching	12
Tuesday's Gone	16
The Ballad Of Curtis Loew	20
I Need You	24
Travellin' Man	28
Simple Man	32
Saturday Night Special	41
Whiskey Rock-A-Roller	44
Sweet Home Alabama	48
On The Hunt	53
Don't Ask Me No Questions	56
Cry For The Bad Man	61
Gimme Three Steps	64
The Needle And The Spoon	68
Call Me The Breeze	70
Double Trouble	77
Blue Yodel ("T" For Texas)	82
Gimme Back My Bullets	86
Free Bird	90

© 1977 Universal-MCA Music Publishing, a Division of Universal Studios, Inc.
All Rights Reserved

Foreword

That the better part of contemporary popular music has its roots in the American South is a statement that will bring little argument from most students of the art; that the prime example of that region's musical influence during the course of the '70s has been a group of musicians known collectively as Lynyrd Skynyrd is an assertion that will bring even less argument in decades to come.

In the short span of three years since their now legendary debut in Atlanta before a crowd of record industry executives, disc jockeys and press, these native Floridians have compiled a track record that almost defies comparison. Each of their five MCA albums, from the prototypical "Pronounced 'Leh-'nerd 'Skin-'nerd" to the current "One More From The Road," has been destined for gold certification from day of release, and each has accumulated such vast amounts of airplay that one can scarcely drive through any city, regardless of its locale, without being exposed to their boilermaker brand of rock.

But the proof of Lynyrd Skynyrd's magic goes beyond record sales and airplay. The group's constant touring — a seemingly endless string of SRO dates — provides crowds from coast to coast and beyond with a brand of music that bursts with the raw power and vitality of southern-style rock 'n' roll.

Once beheld on stage, Skynyrd leaves a lasting impression on the senses, one that shines through uncounted listening bouts with their lps: Ronnie Van Zant, the original Peck's Bad Boy, strutting barefoot across the stage, exhorting guitarists Allen Collins, Gary Rossington and Steve Gaines on to higher and higher levels of energy; Leon Wilkeson grinning confidently from behind his bass; Artimus Pyle pounding out solid southern backbeats on his drums; and keyboardist Billy Powell burning up the audience with riffs that belie his quiet demeanor.

Indeed, while their career is still in its youthful stages, the members of Lynyrd Skynyrd have achieved a collective level of prominence that few groups ever hope to attain. And if, by some remote chance, you have yet to experience the joys of their music, you might do well to heed the words of Ronnie Van Zant in 'Things Goin' On":

"If you don't know what I mean
Won't you stand up and scream
'Cause there's things goin' on
You don't know"

Howard Levitt
Associate Editor
Record World

ADDITIONAL LYRICS

Verse 2
    Oh, nine thousand dollars just to sow to the wind
    Come to smile at the yankee slicker with a big old southern grin.
    They're gonna take me out to California, gonna make me a super star.
    Just pay me all my money mister you want me a star.

    Repeat Chorus

Verse 3
    Slickers steal my money since I was seventeen
    If it ain't no pencil pusher then it got to be a honky tonk queen
    But I signed my contract baby, and I want you people to know
    That every penny that I make, I gotta see where my money goes.

    Repeat Chorus

I Ain't The One

Words and Music by
ALLEN COLLINS and RONNIE VAN ZANT

© 1973, 1976 Universal - Duchess Music Corporation and EMI Longitude Music
All Rights Controlled and Administered by Universal - Duchess Music Corporation
All Rights Reserved

Verse 2.
    Now you're talkin' jive, woman,
    When you say to me
    Your daddy's gonna take us in
    'N take care of me.
    You know and I know, woman
    I ain't the one.
    I never hurt you, sweetheart
    I never pulled my gun
    Got bells in your mind, mama
    And it's easy to see
    I think it's time for me to move along
    I do believe.

Searching

Words and Music by
ALLEN COLLINS and RONNIE VAN ZANT

© 1976 Universal - Duchess Music Corporation and Get Loose Music, Inc.
All Rights Controlled and Administered by Universal - Duchess Music Corporation
All Rights Reserved

ADDITIONAL LYRICS

Verse 3.
    You can have anything in this God's world
    But you won't be happy son, til you find a girl
    Now you can be happy, boy, if you try
    Find a woman boy, you'll be satisfied

Repeat Chorus

Tuesday's Gone

Words and Music by
ALLEN COLLINS and RONNIE VAN ZANT

© 1973, 1978 Universal - Duchess Music Corporation and Get Loose Music, Inc.
All Rights Controlled and Administered by Universal - Duchess Music Corporation
All Rights Reserved

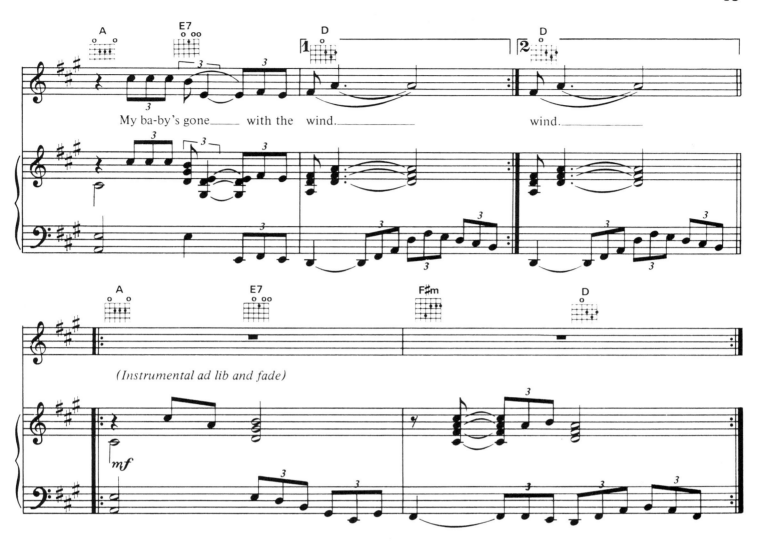

Verse 3.
    Train roll on many miles from my home
    See I'm riding my blues away
    Tuesday, you see, she had to be free,
    But somehow, I've got to carry on.

The Ballad Of Curtis Loew

Words and Music by
ALLEN COLLINS and RONNIE VAN ZANT

© 1974, 1977 Universal - Duchess Music Corporation and EMI Longitude Music
All Rights Controlled and Administered by Universal - Duchess Music Corporation
All Rights Reserved

ADDITIONAL LYRICS

Verse 2.
    He looked to be sixty, maybe I was ten
    Mama used to whip me but I'd go see him again
    I'd clap my hands, stomp my feet, try to stay in time
    He'd play me a song or two,
    Then take another drink of wine.

Chorus

Verse 3.
    On the day old Curtis died, nobody came to pray
    Old preacher said some words and they chunked him in the clay
    But he lived a lifetime playin' the black face blues
    And on the day he lost his life
    That's all he had to lose.

Repeat Chorus

Verse 2.
    I woke up early this mornin' and the sun came shining down
    And it found me wishin' and hopin' mama, you could be around
    For you know I need you more than the air I breathe
    And I guess I'm tryin' to tell you mama,
    What you mean to me.

    Repeat Chorus

Verse 3.
    I'm tryin' to tell you I love you in each and every way
    I'm tryin' to tell you I need you
    Much more than just a piece of lay.

    Repeat Chorus

Travellin' Man

Words and Music by
RONNIE VAN ZANT and LEON WILKESON

© 1976 Universal - Duchess Music Corporation and Get Loose Music, Inc.
All Rights Controlled and Administered by Universal - Duchess Music Corporation
All Rights Reserved

ADDITIONAL LYRICS

Verse 2
    Trav'lin' man, that's what I am
    Mama puts a load on me
    You see me once or maybe twice
    That's all you'll see of me
    All you pretty women
    Lord, I hope you understand
    Don't be fallin' in love
    Just call in a trav'lin' man.

Verse 3
    Trav'lin' man, that's what I am
    Lord, I move so fast
    I have had so many women
    None of them have last
    I am a steady mover
    Movin' fast as sound
    Always be some time for
    Always movin' around.

Verse 3.
    Forget your lust for rich man's gold
    All that you need is in your soul.
    And you can do this if you try
    All that I want for you, my son
    Is to be satisfied.

Verse 4.
    Boy, don't you worry . . . you'll find yourself
    Follow your heart and nothing else.
    And you can do this if you try.
    All that I want for you, my son
    Is to be satisfied.

Repeat Chorus

Steve Gaines

Ronnie Van Zant

Allen Collins   Gary Rossington

Billy Powell

Saturday Night Special

Words and Music by
EDWARD KING and RONNIE VAN ZANT

ADDITIONAL LYRICS

Verse 2.
    Big Jim's been drinkin' whiskey
    And playin' poker on a losin' night
    Pretty soon big Jim starts a-thinkin'
    Somebody been cheatin' and lyin'
    So big Jim commences to fightin'
    I wouldn't tell you no lie.
    And big Jim done pulled his pistol
    Shot his friend right between the eyes.

Repeat Chorus

Verse 3.
    Hand guns are made for killin'
    Ain't no good for nothin' else
    And if you like to drink your whiskey
    You might even shoot yourself
    So why don't we dump them people
    To the bottom of the sea.
    Before some fool come around here
    Wanna shoot either you or me.

ADDITIONAL LYRICS

Verse 2.
    I was born a travellin' man and my feets do burn the ground.
    I don't care for fancy music if your shoes can't shuffle around
    I got a hundred women or more and there's no place I call home
    The only time I'm satisfied is when I'm on the road.

    Repeat Chorus

Verse 3.
    Take me down to Memphis town, bus driver get me there
    I got me a queenie, she got long brown curly hair
    She likes to drink old Grandad and her shoes do shuffle around
    And every time I see that girl, Lord she wants to lay me down.

    Repeat Chorus

Sweet Home Alabama

Words and Music by
RONNIE VAN ZANT, ED KING
and GARY ROSSINGTON

© 1974 Universal - Duchess Music Corporation and EMI Longitude Music
All Rights Controlled and Administered by Universal - Duchess Music Corporation
All Rights Reserved

ADDITIONAL LYRICS

Verse 4. Now Muscle Shoals has got the Swampers
And they've been known to pick a tune or two
Lord they get me off so much
They pick me up when I'm feeling blue
Now how about you.

Repeat Chorus and Fade

ADDITIONAL LYRICS

Verse 2.
    I said lady, I know people gonna talk about you and me
    But let me say one thing, sugar, I do as I please.
    And if you wanna love me baby, I'm you're man
    And all those high-falutin' society people
    I don't care if they don't understand.

    Repeat Chorus

Verse 3.
    My daddy told me a long time ago
    Said, there's two things son, two things you should know
    And in these two things, you must take pride
    And that's a horse and a woman, yeah,
    Well, both of them you ride.

    Repeat Chorus

Don't Ask Me No Questions

Words and Music by
RONNIE VAN ZANT and GARY ROSSINGTON

© 1974, 1978 Universal - Duchess Music Corporation and EMI Longitude Music
All Rights Controlled and Administered by Universal - Duchess Music Corporation
All Rights Reserved

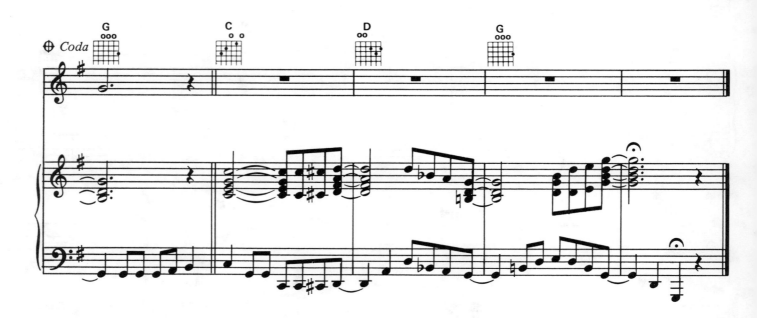

ADDITIONAL LYRICS

Verse 3.
    Well, what's your favorite color
    And do you dig the Brothers
    Drivin' me up the wall.

    And every time I think I can sleep
    Some fool has got to call

    Well don't you think that when I
    Come home I just want a
    Little piece of mind.

    If you want to talk about the
    Business buddy you're just wasting time.

Cry For The Bad Man

Words and Music by
GARY ROSSINGTON, ALLEN COLLINS
and RONNIE VAN ZANT

© 1976 Universal - Duchess Music Corporation and Get Loose Music, Inc.
All Rights Controlled and Administered by Universal - Duchess Music Corporation
All Rights Reserved

ADDITIONAL LYRICS

Verse 2.
    Well you treat me right and I'll treat you right
    That's the way it's supposed to be
    But I put my faith down in my friend
    And he almost put an end to me.

    Well I work seven days a week
    And eight when I'm able
    And when you take my money from me
    You take food from my momma's table.

    Repeat Chorus

Verse 3.
    Well treat me right and I'll treat you right
    That's the way it's supposed to be
    But I put my faith down in my friend
    And he almost put an end to me.

    Well when you take my money, baby
    When you hurt my family
    It's like walkin' through the swamps without no shoes
    And step on a snake, it's deadly.

    Repeat Chorus

Verse 3.
    Well, the crowd cleared away, and I began to pray
        and the water fell on the floor.
    And I'm telling you son, it ain't no fun staring
        straight down a forty four
    Well, he turned and screamed at Linda Lu
        and that's the break I was looking for.
    And you could hear me screaming a mile away
        As I was headed out toward the door.

Repeat Chorus

The Needle And The Spoon

Verse 3.
    I've seen alot of people who thought they were cool
    But then again, Lord, I've seen alot of fools.
    I hope you people Lord can hear what I say
    You'll have your chance in this some day.

Chorus
    Don't mess with a needle, or a spoon, or a trip to the moon
    Or they'll take you away.

ADDITIONAL LYRICS

Verse 2.
    Well, I got that green light, baby
    I got to keep movin' on
    Well, I got that green light, baby
    I got to keep movin' on
    Well I might go out to California
    Might go down to Georgia, I don't know.

Verse 3.
    Well, I dig you Georgia peaches
    Makes me feel right at home
    Well, I dig you Georgia peaches
    Makes me feel right at home
    But I don't love me no one woman
    So I can't stay in Georgia long.

Gary Rossington

Artimus Pyle

Leon Wilkeson

Allen Collins

Double Trouble

Words and Music by
ALLEN COLLINS and RONNIE VAN ZANT

© 1976 Universal - Duchess Music Corporation and Get Loose Music, Inc.
All Rights Controlled and Administered by Universal - Duchess Music Corporation
All Rights Reserved

ADDITIONAL LYRICS

Verse 3.

I was born down in the gutter
with a temper hot as fire.
Spent ninety days on a pea farm
doin' the county's time.
Even Mama says
Son you're bad news. *(Answer: Born to lose.)*
And it won't be too long 'for
someone puts one through you.
Repeat Chorus.

Blue Yodel ("T" For Texas)

Words and Music by
JIMMY RODGERS

© 1928 by PEER INTERNATIONAL CORPORATION
© Renewed 1955 by PEER INTERNATIONAL CORPORATION
All Rights Reserved   Used by Permission

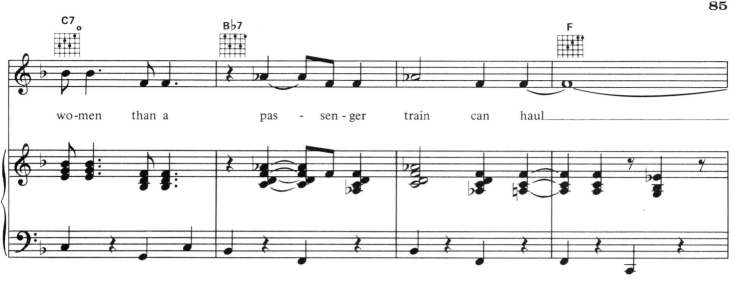

ADDITIONAL LYRICS

Verse 3.
    I'm gonna buy myself a shotgun
    One with a long shiny barrel
    Gonna buy myself a shotgun
    One with a long shiny barrel
    I'm goin' shoot myself a rounder
    Oh, that stole away my gal.

Verse 4.
    I'm gonna drink your muddy water
    Sleep down in a hollow log
    I'm gonna drink your muddy water
    Sleep down in a hollow log
    If you been in the land of Georgia
    Treated like a dirty dog.

ADDITIONAL LYRICS

3rd Verse.
    Been up and down since I turned seventeen
    Well I've been on top then it seems I lost my dream
    But I've got it back I'm feeling better every day
    Tell all those pencil pushers better get outa my way.

Repeat Chorus

Free Bird

Words and Music by
ALLEN COLLINS and RONNIE VAN ZANT

If I leave here to-mor-row, Would you still re-mem-ber
Bye, bye ba-by it's been a sweet love though this feel-ing I can't

me? For I must be trav-'ling on now
change. But please don't take it so bad-ly

© 1973, 1975 Universal - Duchess Music Corporation and EMI Longitude Music
All Rights Controlled and Administered by Universal - Duchess Music Corporation
All Rights Reserved

Leslie Hawkins   Cassie Gaines   Jo Billingsley

Two Former Members
Ed King

Bob Burns